W9-AVD-173

REPTILES
AND AMPHIBIANS
STICKER ACTIVITY BOOK

Pull out the sticker sheets and keep them by you as you complete each page. There are also lots of extra stickers to use in this book or anywhere you want! Have fun!

NATIONAL GEOGRAPHIC
Washington, D.C.

Consultant: Mark O'Shea
Editorial, Design, and Production by

make believe ideas

Picture credits: All images Shutterstock unless noted as follows:
©Andrew Murray/naturepl.com: 27 ml (goliath frog), ©Bert Willaert/naturepl.com:
26 tl (Darwin's frog), Dreamstime: 2 ml (Madagascar day gecko), 7 tl (fire salamander), 17 tr
(green sea turtle), 20 tl (young American alligator), 36 bl (American bullfrog), Jak Wonderly/NGS:
40 br (pond slider turtle), Make Believe Ideas: 8 ml; mr, 9 ml (sea star x3), 8 ml, 9 ml (sea shell x3),
10 br (mouse x2), 16 ml, 17 tr; bl (small yellow fish x3), NGS: 6 tl (frog spawn), Paul Tessier/iStock:
6 tr (python with eggs), Walter Meayers Edwards/NGC: 39 ml (diamondback rattlesnake).

Sticker pages: All images Shutterstock unless noted as follows: ©Bert Willaert/naturepl.com:
26, 27 Darwin's frog x5, Bianca Lavies/NGC: 4, 5 leaping pickerel frog, Chris Johns/NGC: 14, 15 Jackson's
chameleon (bl), Dreamstime: 4, 5 fire salamander (tl), 6, 7 poison dart frog x4, 14, 15 thorny devil lizard (m),
20, 21 American alligators (t), 26, 27 dyeing poison frog (l), 40 sea turtle, Extra Stickers (Sheet3) leopard frog x15,
Extra Stickers (Sheet 4) fire salamander x12, Extra Stickers (Sheet 8) leopard frog x10, poison dart frog x8,
Gary Nafis: 34, 35 rough-skinned newt (tl), Jak Wonderly/NGS: 6, 7 tortoise, 12, 13 leopard gecko x5, 18, 19
African spur-thighed tortoise (ml), Make Believe Ideas: 8, 9 sea shell x2; sea star x2, 10, 11 mouse, 16, 17
small red fish x3; small colorful fish x3, 28, 29 fly x3, Extra Stickers (Sheet 4) sea shell x6; sea star x3,
Extra stickers (sheet 8) fly x19, Matt Propert/NGS: 10, 11 mr red mountain rat snake.

Printed in China. 16/MBI/1

Snakes, lizards, geckos, tuataras, turtles, and crocodiles are all types of reptiles!

Color the wiggly snake!

parrot snake

Madagascar day gecko

American alligator

panther chameleon

Find the missing stickers.

Reptiles are cold-blooded. They love to find warm places to rest.

green iguana

Help the turtle get through the maze to her babies!

Start

Finish

snapping turtles

Snapping turtles can't pull their heads into their shells, so they defend themselves with their sharp jaws!

Amphibians need to live near **water.**

red-eyed tree frog

Frogs, toads, and salamanders are all types of amphibians.

American bullfrog

fire salamander

tree frog

Color the newt.

4

Sticker the animals in the right categories.

amphibian

salamander

frog

toad

newt

reptile

Reptiles have waterproof skin, but amphibians breathe through theirs!

snake

tortoise

Color the chameleon.

7

How are reptiles and amphibians **born?**

slimy frog eggs

Reptiles and amphibians are born or hatched from eggs. They don't look like the eggs you get from the store, though!

soft snake eggs

After hatching, baby sea turtles travel from their nest to the ocean.

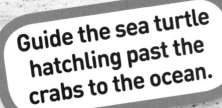

Guide the sea turtle hatchling past the crabs to the ocean.

Some geckos lay their eggs under rocks and in logs to keep their babies safe until they hatch!

Find the 10 gecko babies playing hide-and-seek in this picture. Don't forget, they can stick upside down!

Female pythons coil around their eggs to keep the babies warm and protect them.

9

Snakes are a type of reptile without legs.

There are more than 3,600 species of snake. They are found on every continent but Antarctica!

eastern coral snake

The snake can smell something tasty! Help it through the maze to its dinner.

Start ↓

Finish

The boa constrictor squeezes its prey before eating it!

boa constrictor

The green vine snake lives in bushes and trees.

red mountain rat snake

Decorate the snake with bright colors.

Geckos come in lots of different colors.

leaf-tailed gecko

Geckos lick their eyes to keep them clean!

Trace the trails to find out which kind of gecko lives where.

gold dust day gecko

tokay gecko

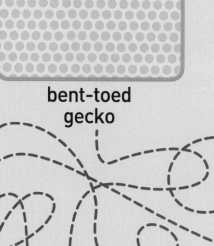
bent-toed gecko

Pakistan

northern Madagascar

southeastern Asia

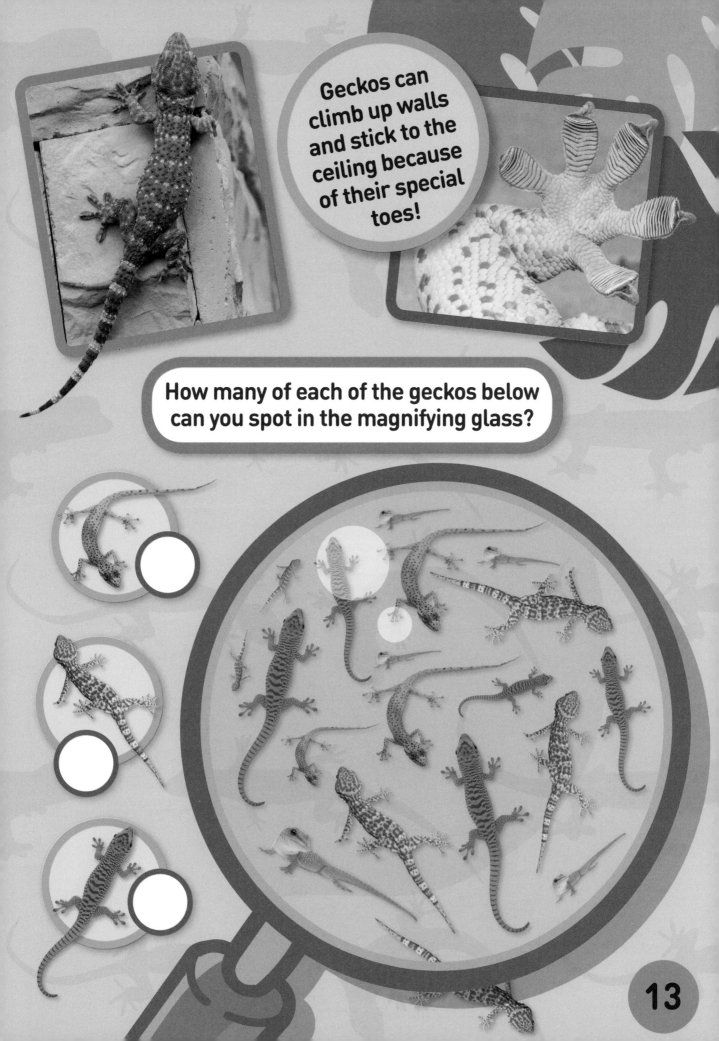

Geckos can climb up walls and stick to the ceiling because of their special toes!

How many of each of the geckos below can you spot in the magnifying glass?

There are more than 6,200 species of **lizard!**

The Komodo dragon is the largest living lizard.

Lizards can detach their tails to escape being caught!

thorny devil lizard

green iguana

Color the Komodo dragon.

Stickers for pages 2 and 3

Stickers for pages 4 and 5

Extra stickers

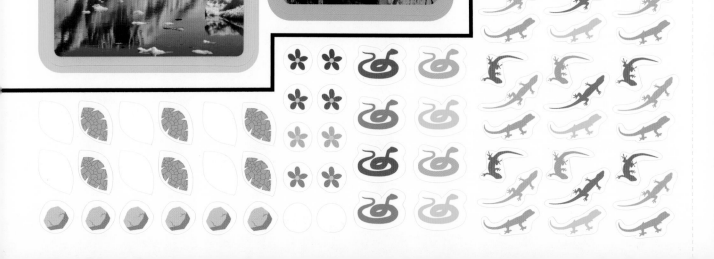

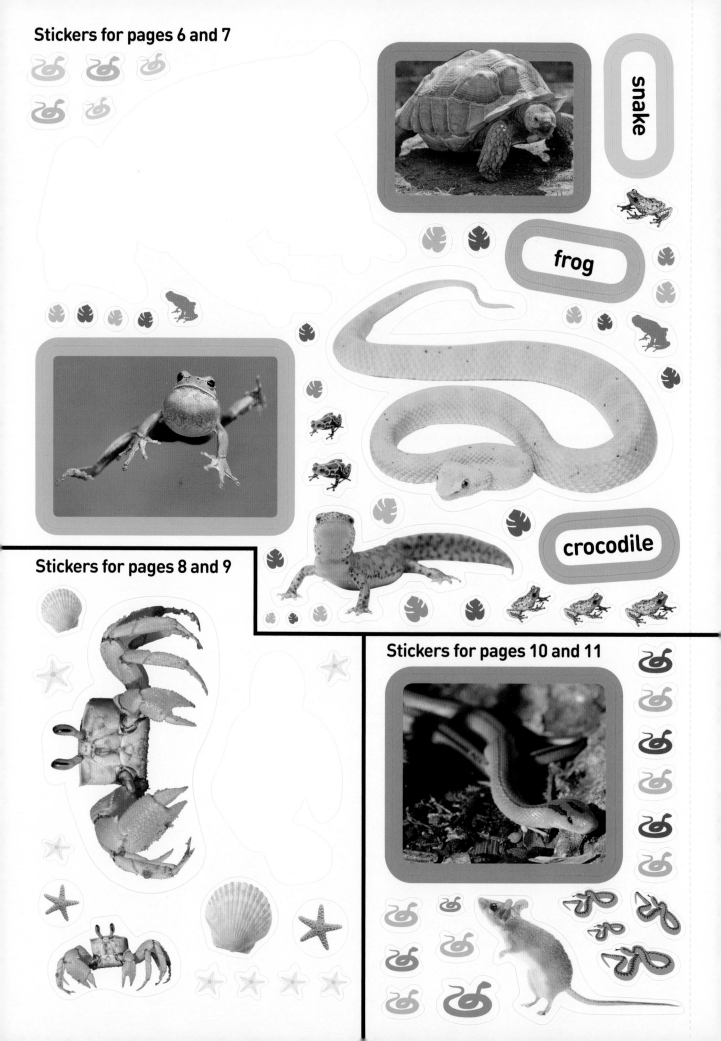

Stickers for pages 6 and 7

snake

frog

crocodile

Stickers for pages 8 and 9

Stickers for pages 10 and 11

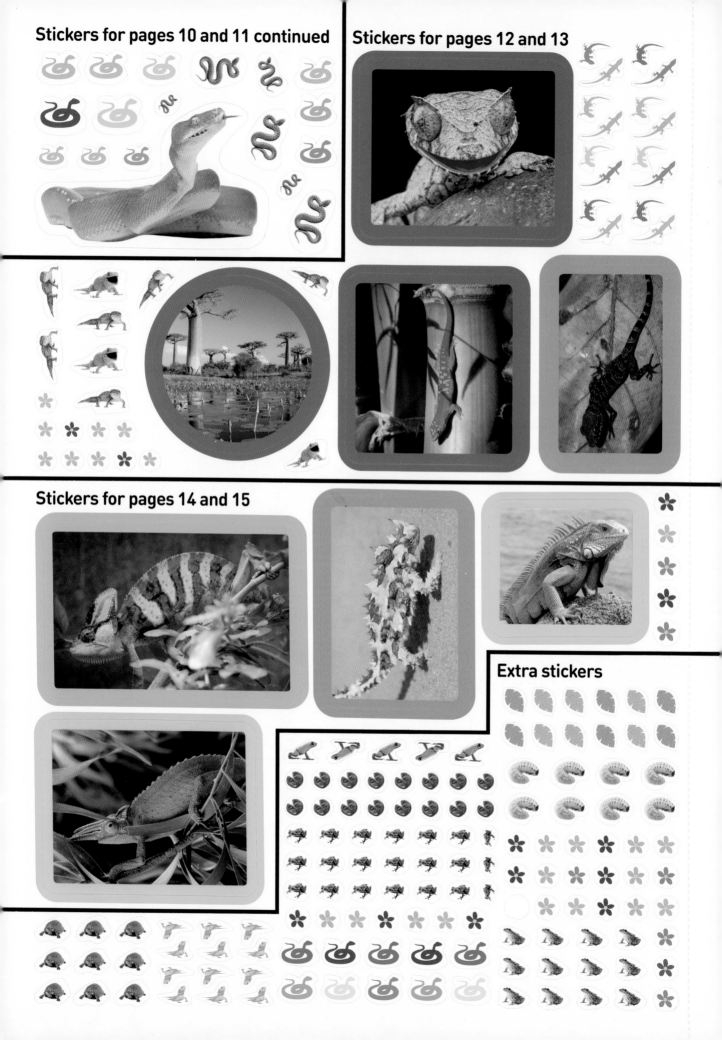

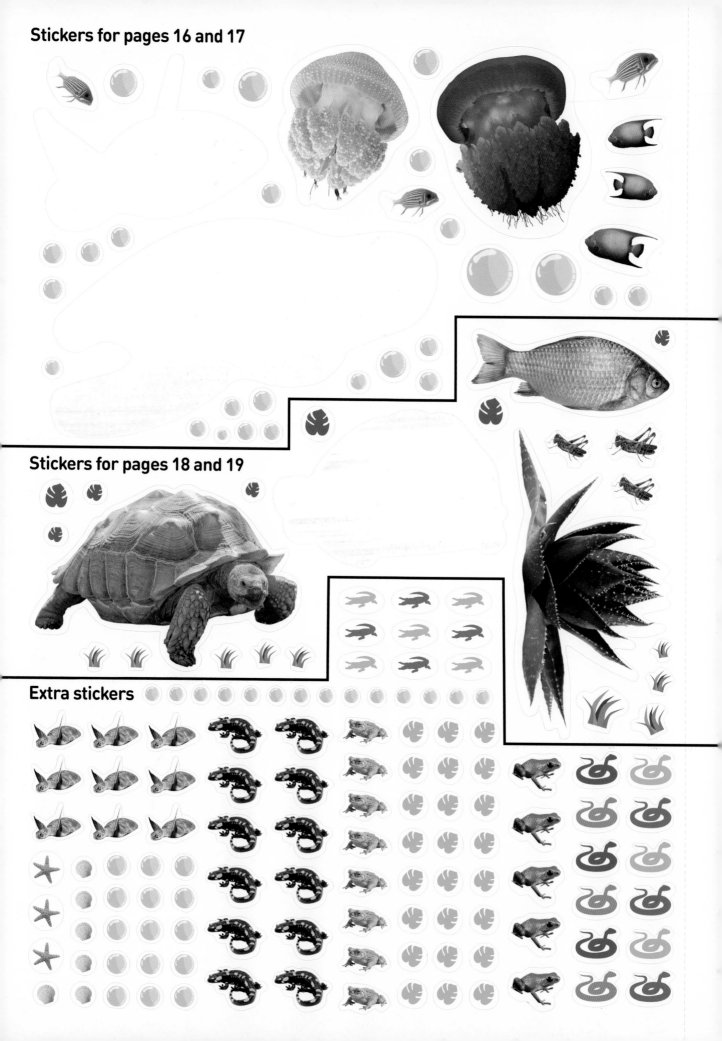

Stickers for pages 16 and 17

Stickers for pages 18 and 19

Extra stickers

Stickers for pages 20 and 21

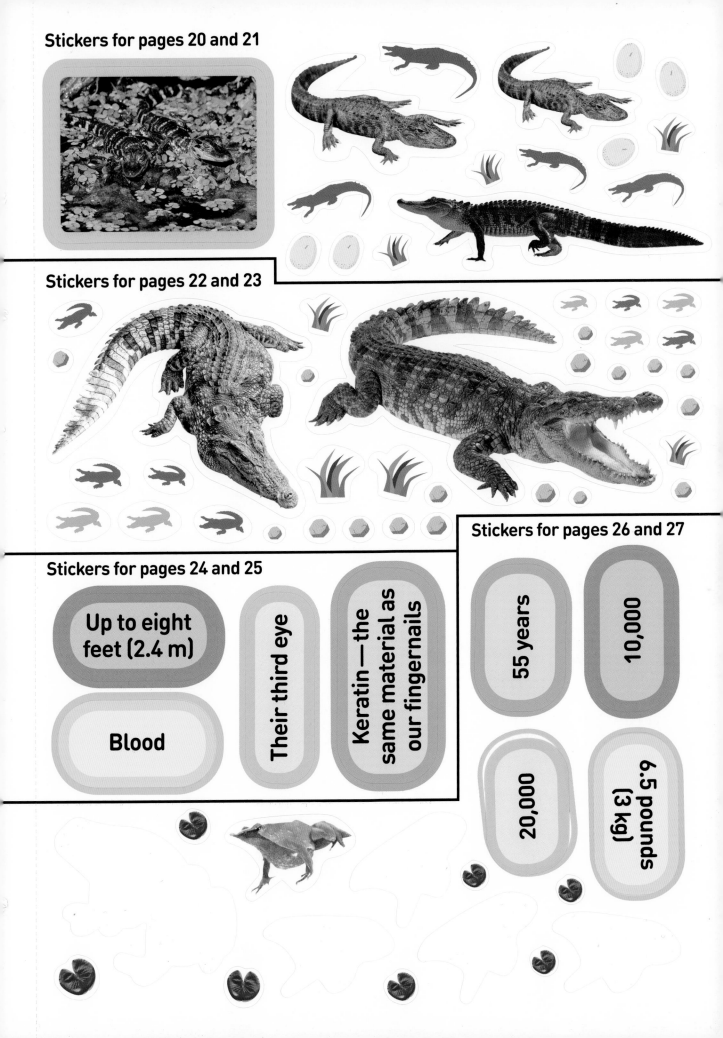

Stickers for pages 22 and 23

Stickers for pages 24 and 25

Up to eight feet (2.4 m)

Blood

Their third eye

Keratin—the same material as our fingernails

Stickers for pages 26 and 27

55 years

10,000

20,000

6.5 pounds (3 kg)

Stickers for pages 28 and 29

Stickers for pages 30 and 31

Stickers for pages 32 and 33

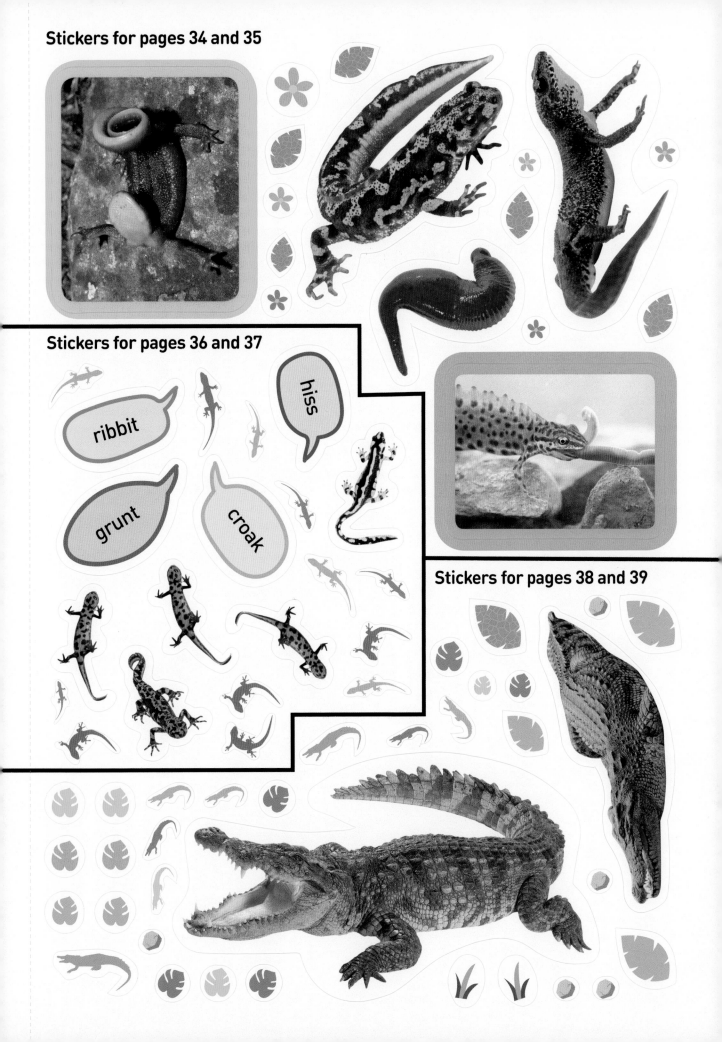

Stickers for pages 34 and 35

Stickers for pages 36 and 37

ribbit

hiss

grunt

croak

Stickers for pages 38 and 39

Stickers for page 40

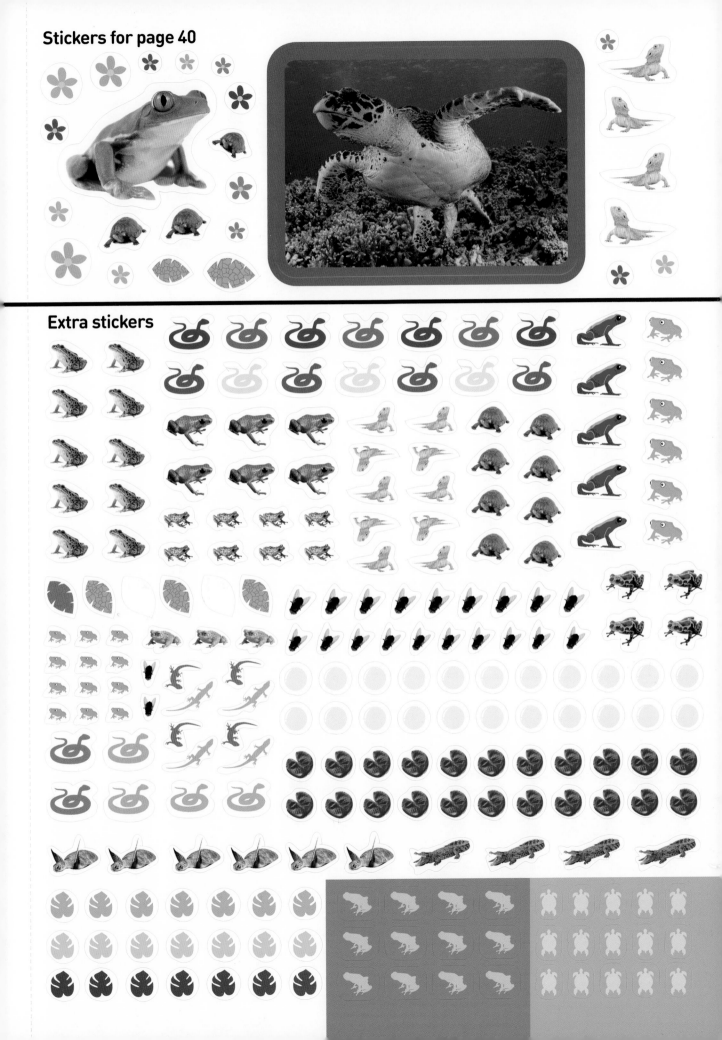

Extra stickers

Using the key, cross the river without running into an alligator.

Key:

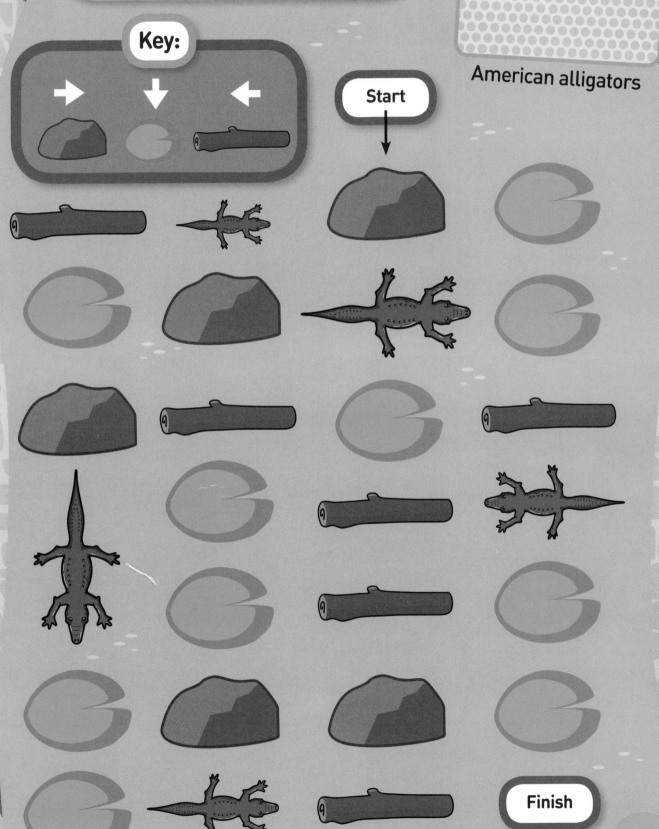

American alligators

Start

Finish

21

Crocodiles are very **fast** swimmers!

Q: How can you tell a crocodile from an alligator?

A: Crocodiles have a bottom tooth that sticks out when their jaw is closed!

Help the crocodile find its friends.

Start

Finish

22

What other amazing things can **reptiles** do?

Most reptiles can survive for long periods without food.

Sticker your answers about these cool reptiles.

How far can cobras spit their venom?

What does the horned lizard squirt from its eyes to confuse predators?

What are snake scales made of?

What helps green iguanas sense predators above them?

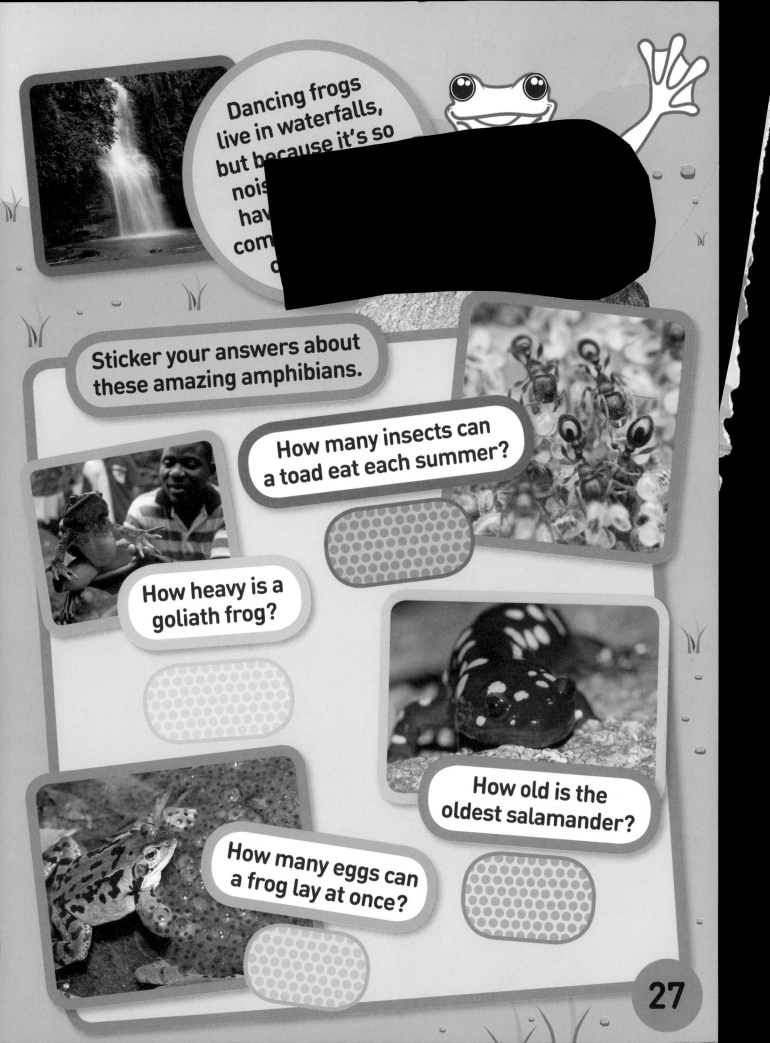

Dancing frogs live in waterfalls, but because it's so nois... hav... com...

Sticker your answers about these amazing amphibians.

How many insects can a toad eat each summer?

How heavy is a goliath frog?

How old is the oldest salamander?

How many eggs can a frog lay at once?

Frogs come in all **shapes** and **sizes**.

How many frogs can you find in the tree?

Find my friends!

28

There are more than 600 species of salamander in the world!

Using your checklist as a guide, count the different salamanders you see.

fire
salamander

marbled
salamander

red
salamander

blue-spotted
salamander

Newts are a kind of salamander.

Some male newts develop large jagged crests on their backs to attract female newts!

great crested newt

Alpine newt

Make the newt's belly bright and colorful to scare away predators!

Rough-skinned newts quickly flash their bright bellies at predators to scare them away. It looks like this!

rough-skinned newt

Newts are carnivores—they can get sick if they eat plants instead of meat!

common newt

marbled newt

Circle the objects that don't belong in the newt's dinner.

No lettuce, please!

mandarin newt

Reptiles and amphibians are so cool!

Newts can regrow missing parts, including their arms, legs, eyes, and even hearts!

Sticker the newts to finish the patterns.

Sticker the noise each animal makes.

gray tree frog

American bullfrog

amphibians

Find all of the places herpetologists work.

aquarium
museum
school
zoo
wild

a	h	e	a	b	p	a	w
r	q	r	n	t	o	m	a
a	q	u	a	r	i	u	m
a	z	a	a	o	a	s	y
e	o	e	n	z	n	e	b
s	c	h	o	o	l	u	a
w	i	l	d	o	p	m	a

The word "herpetology" comes from the Greek word herpeton. It means "to creep"!

Can you say hur-pi-tol-uh-jee?

Which are your **favorites?**

Find the missing stickers.

Draw a picture of the reptile or amphibian you like best.